HOW ARE THEY BUILT?

HOUSES

Lynn M. Stone

Rourke Publishing LLC
Vero Beach, Florida 32964

www.rourkepublishing.com

PHOTO CREDITS:
Cover ©Lynn M. Stone; pages 10, 16, 26, 33, 34, 37, 41, 43 ©Armentrout; pages 4, 8, 14 ©James P. Rowan; page 39 ©Dynamic Design; page 29 © AP/Wide World; pages 11, 12, 19, 20, 23, 24 ©Photo Disc, Inc.

EDITORIAL SERVICES:
Pamela Schroeder

ABOUT THE AUTHOR
Lynn Stone is the author of more than 400 children's books. He is a talented natural history photographer as well. Lynn, a former teacher, travels worldwide to photograph wildlife in its natural habitat.

Library of Congress Cataloging-in-Publication Data

Stone, Lynn M.
    Houses / Lynn M. Stone
        p. cm. — (How are they built?)
    Includes bibliographical references and index.
    Summary: Discusses house construction in the United States, in the past as well as the present.
        ISBN 1-58952-137-4
        1. Housing construction—Juvenile literature. 2. Dwellings—Juvenile literature. [1. House construction. 2. Dwellings. 3. Building.] I. Stone, Lynn M. How are they Built? II. Title.

TH4811.5 .S76 2001
690'.837'0973—dc21   2001041646

Printed In The USA

TABLE OF CONTENTS

The homes of the earliest English settlers in North America were made of wood and clay with roofs of thatch.

HOUSES

The first houses built by European settlers in North America were little more than shelters. Many were one- or two-room structures built with wood and mud. They had roofs of **thatch**, dried reeds tied into a bushy mat.

North American homes have grown bigger and better since European settlers set up housekeeping in Jamestown, Virginia (1607); Plymouth, Massachusetts (1620); and Boston (1630). In fact, housing in North America is a business worth billions of dollars and affecting millions of people.

People in housing are not only designers and builders. They are also **architects**, excavators, carpenters, roofers, siders, painters, plumbers, tilers, and **contractors**, among others. There are people who make the materials used in housing, such as concrete, paint, electrical wire, wood, brick, **asphalt**, tile, glass, plaster, gypsum, and aluminum. And remember the millions of people who buy houses and the thousands of banks that lend money to them.

Houses have changed, but their purpose is the same now as it was 400 years ago—to provide shelter, privacy, and comfort. Early Americans would be amazed at all the sizes, styles, materials, and locations of today's houses. And the comfort of modern houses would be sure to wow them!

HISTORY OF HOUSES

As English settlers on the east coast survived their first harsh winter or two, they began to build better houses. Most of the first houses were made of wood. Wood was everywhere, so it was an easy choice for a building material. Most settlers already knew how to use wood from their experience in England.

Rough-sawn plank walls were typical of the cottage homes in old New England. Even chimney frames were wooden!

Brick homes would not become common until after 1700. The **colonists** had seen few brick homes in England, and brick homes need mortar to seal the bricks together. Mortar is a mixture of lime, sand, and water. During the colonists' time, lime was difficult to get. As far as anyone knows, only eight brick homes were built in New England before 1700.

Early homes were simple cottages. They had walls made of split logs and roofs of wood shingles or thatch. The colonists filled wall cracks with clay. Windows were small. Because glass was expensive and hard to get, "windows" were made of linen treated with oil. Their fireplaces had wooden chimneys, although they were covered with clay. The clay, however, could flake off. With wooden chimneys and thatch roofs, these homes caught fire easily. Local laws soon stopped the use of such fire-friendly roofs and chimneys.

Many of the early American houses had two rooms in front and a third in the rear. The simplest houses had one downstairs room with a fireplace. A ladder led to an attic or sleeping loft, built under the house's steeply sloped roof. The main room served as an adult bedroom, dining room, living room, and kitchen.

Swedish colonists built the first true log cabins in North America. Notice the stone chimney, an improvement over wood.

Seventeenth-century houses in America were a lot like the houses the colonists had known in England. The colonists did not invent new building techniques or styles. But they did begin to build larger houses for themselves, such as the saltbox. The saltbox house was a common kind of house in England by the end of the 1500s. Colonists brought the style to America. The saltbox had a very long, sloping rear roof. It provided more space on the first floor. In Delaware, Swedish colonists built the first true log cabins in North America in 1638. Later, log cabins became the most common kind of home as Americans moved west.

As the colonies grew, many of the colonists became wealthy. They used their wealth to build better houses. None of the early thatch-and-split-log houses has survived. But many of the 17th and 18th-century homes of wealthy and middle-class colonists have.

In the 1700s, wealthy colonists began building homes of the Georgian style. English architects borrowed the style from Andrea Palladio and the Italian **Renaissance**. By 1700, the Georgian style had reached the American colonies in manuals and style books.

American colonists began to build houses that showed strong influences from Italy and France as well as from England.

11

The Georgian house eliminated the sloping back roof of the New England saltbox home and added a new style to American houses.

Georgian-style houses don't have the sloping, lean-to look of the saltbox. In Georgian houses the back of the house is the same height as the front. **Symmetry**, evenness, was important in Georgian houses. The front door was in the middle with the same number of rooms and windows on each side. Above each downstairs room and window was a matching upstairs room and window. Colonists who could afford them wanted big, elegant Georgian houses. In larger cities like Newport, Rhode Island; Williamsburg, Virginia; Portsmouth, New Hampshire; and Charleston, South Carolina, colonists built huge Georgian houses. Instead of houses with two or three rooms, the Georgians had four or five rooms per floor! In addition to bedrooms, these houses had a separate kitchen, library, dining room, formal room or parlor, and banquet room.

This Chicago Prairie style home illustrates the long, straight lines and low roofs typical of the style.

By 1780, the Georgian style of **architecture** gave way to the similar, but more refined, Federalist, or Adam style. This was another style from England. Even though the United States had just defeated England in the Revolutionary War, the new nation did not turn its back on British architecture! Federalist architecture was popular into the 1820s.

In the years that followed, many new styles of architecture came to America. One of the most interesting was the Queen Anne style. It began shortly after the Civil War (1861-1865). The Queen Anne style was very different from the even Georgian and Federalist styles. Queen Anne houses were full of points and angles. They had tall, sloping slate roofs, different-sized porches, **gables**, bay windows, fancy shingles, patterned **masonry**, and outdoor **spindlework**. They were painted in bright colors.

In Chicago, late in the 19th century, a style known as the Chicago Prairie style began. Frank Lloyd Wright, the most famous of American architects, used this style. The Prairie style, with its long, straight lines, low roofs, and tall windows affected architecture throughout the world. The style was used mostly in the Midwest.

Most American house styles follow one of four main kinds of architecture. They are Ancient Classical, Renaissance Classical, Medieval, and Modern, which began in the late 19th century.

Most people today want a house that suits their style of living. They don't build houses that follow a single architectural style. Most American homes built since 1965 are what some architects call "neo-eclectic"—a new blend of many styles.

*Many new American homes are a blend of several
old architectural styles.*

WHO BUILDS HOUSES?

A buyer, family, contractor, or land developer may
have a house built. An individual or family usually builds
a house in which they plan to live. A contractor or land
developer may build a house without knowing who the
buyer will be. The idea is that someone will like the
house and buy it from the builder. This is called building
on **speculation**, or "spec."

Anyone who builds needs a plan for the house. An architect draws those plans, based on what the buyer wants. It is the architect's job to see that the house can be built the way the buyer would like. The architect has to create a plan so the house structure will be strong and meet all local building laws.

The construction of the house is arranged by a contractor. The contractor determines the costs and gets the building materials. Material costs vary from week to week, like gasoline prices. Some building materials may be difficult to find, so careful planning is important. Contractors also hire the people who will complete the job. These are carpenters, electricians, plumbers, roofers, and others, all of whom are called **subcontractors**. In most cases, the contractor does not construct any of the house. He or she organizes the construction. Building a home requires the contractor's attention every day. Each step of the building process depends upon the one before.

During the construction, the work is checked from time to time by a building inspector. The inspector works for the city or county. The inspector makes sure that the subcontractors' work is meeting the local building laws.

The price of a house varies with its size, style, and location. A home located in southern California would not cost the same as the same kind of home in Houston, Texas. California homes are usually more expensive.

Houses in and close to big cities were often built extremely close together to conserve land. They are called row houses.

A large, formal house like this is often called a mansion or manor house.

KINDS OF HOUSES

Many people label houses in terms of size. Small houses may be called bungalows or cottages. The largest, most formal houses are mansions. But there are many ways to name houses. One refers to how many families a house is built to hold. Traditional American houses are single-family homes. They are built as homes for one family. Duplexes are "twin" houses that share a common wall. A family lives in each of the two halves. Townhouses, or row houses, include several attached houses, usually two stories high.

Apartment houses don't look like traditional houses at all. They can be huge, high-rises with hundreds of families. Condominiums, or condos, are like apartments, but may be used for rentals or vacations.

Houses are also described by their building materials, such as wood, concrete, brick, or stone. They are described by their architectural styles, too. America has had an unusual number of house styles since the settlers began building. Many groups rebuilt homes of the European styles they had known. Many of those styles were gradually changed by American builders because they had different building materials and their own tastes. America has been a melting pot of cultures, and it has also become a melting pot of architectural styles. Today, more than ever, American houses are a mixed bag of English, French, Italian, Dutch, Spanish, Greek, and Oriental styles.

Where houses are built has always had a great deal to do with their style. The Spanish, adobe-style homes of the Southwest are much different than the Cape Cod and Colonial houses of New England or the wooden ranch homes of the Pacific Coast. Of course, some houses are not built in any style of architecture. They are simply "folk" houses, built for shelter, not for fashion.

Wood was not plentiful in the dry Southwest, so early houses were often built of adobe—sun-baked clay.

This home was built using gravity as a natural snow remover.
Homes in heavy snow areas cannot be built with low sloping roofs.

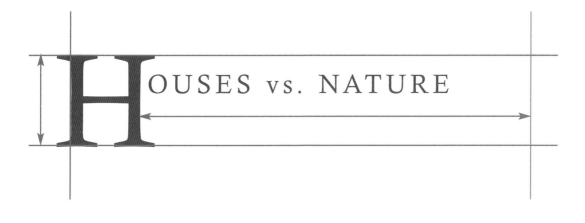

HOUSES vs. NATURE

The two biggest natural forces that home designers plan for are **gravity** and wind. Gravity is the force that tugs on us, that keeps us on the ground. Gravity makes us feel weight. Houses have to be built in ways that manage the effects of weight.

The concrete basement walls of this house will support the weight of the house, furniture, and people that will be above them.

A house has to support its own weight and the **load** of objects brought into it, like furniture and people. A roof, for example, could collapse from its own weight if it were not properly constructed. People figured out long ago that a roof of one size needs the right number of **rafters** at the right size to support it. The idea is to build the house with supports that can handle the weight of just about anything.

Each region of the country has its own laws about house construction. Roofs in Buffalo, New York, for example, are built to carry greater weight than roofs in Miami. Buffalo's snow weighs far more than Miami's rain.

As you look at the skeleton and foundation of a house, you can see how each part supports another. Rafters take the roof weight, but they need some place to take it to. Rafters transfer weight to vertical wooden wall beams called studs. Studs transfer weight down to the house's concrete foundation. The foundation and its **footings**, which you will learn more about later, transfer the weight to the ground. Solid ground has no problem holding firm. Swampy ground or soft soil cannot handle the weight. In this kind of ground houses settle, or sink slowly deeper into the soil.

Built into any house are wood and steel beams. Each house has a different number of beams, but their purpose is the same. They transfer the house's weight above ground into the ground. Simple house plans make the home designer's job easy. Houses with open, airy designs are more difficult since there are fewer support walls.

Wind blows through bridge and roller coaster frames because they are open. Houses, on the other hand, block wind. So house walls have to resist wind. To do that, they are made stronger than they need to be. This helps them to manage both gravity and wind.

It is not likely that anything, except a tornado, can blow a modern house down. In hurricane areas, however, houses are built with extra care. Builders use more shingle nails and add more plywood to the rafters. They also use steel to strap the roof rafters to the walls and the walls to the foundation. Hurricane winds get inside a home and will lift up on a structure. The extra nails and the steel straps help hold things together when wind tries to suck them apart.

Older homes, like this one, are more prone to hurricane damage.
Newer building codes may prevent this kind of damage in the future.

Traditional houses, no matter how well they are built, are no match for the whirling, 300-mile (480-km) per hour winds of a tornado. The best defense in the event of a tornado is to find an underground location.

House designers also have to understand how building materials change with the weather. Summer moisture, for example, makes wood expand, or swell. During cold winters, dry air makes wood contract, or shrink. Wood expanding and contracting can cause cracking or movement in parts of the building.

Moisture can be a problem, too, if it collects in places where it cannot escape. Tarpaper, plastic wraps, and drains are all designed to prevent house moisture problems.

BUILDING A HOUSE

Construction of a house can begin when the building plans are ready and **permits** have been issued by the county or city. Even though houses look different, the way they are built remains basically the same. Here's how a typical one-family home with a basement is built.

The first workers on the new construction site have to clear the land. In wooded lots workers cut down trees and then bulldoze the brush. With an open space, **surveyors** can measure and mark exactly where the house will be built. After the area is marked, the excavator can dig a hole for the home's foundation.

An excavator uses a machine with a scoop to excavate, or remove, dirt from the hole in which the foundation will be built. A house with a basement has a much deeper excavation than a house that will be built upon a concrete slab.

After the excavation, holes or trenches are dug for footings. Footings are concrete supports for the house walls, including the walls of the basement, or cellar. The footings are set below the frost line. That's the level at which frost can freeze the ground. The frost level in northern Minnesota, for example, is much deeper than the frost level in Chicago or Cincinnati. Frost can move earth upward, and that could crack or even lift footings if they were within the reach of ground frost.

An excavator shovels dirt from a basement excavation into a mound.

These forms will be set up to hold liquid concrete
that will harden into basement walls.

Footings are made by pouring concrete into steel or wood forms. The forms work like ceramic molds. The poured concrete hardens in the shape of the form. Then the forms are removed. With footings in place, concrete workers set up new forms for the home's foundation walls, which are usually 8 – 9 feet (2.4 – 2.7 m) tall. The upper level of the walls peaks from about several inches to 3 feet (1 m) above ground level. Again, workers fill the forms with concrete, which is allowed to harden for a few days. Some foundations are made of concrete blocks instead of poured concrete.

While a deep basement foundation is common in the North, it is not in the South. Most houses there are built on concrete slabs. In coastal areas where hurricanes and flooding occur, new houses are built on tall concrete supports called piers. If sea water comes ashore, it washes under the house instead of into it.

Carpenters begin building a house's frame after the concrete foundation is hard and dry. The frame is the skeleton of the house. The walls, floors, and roof will be attached to the frame.

The frame is attached to the foundation walls one step at a time. First, steel sill plates are bolted to the foundation wall tops. The sills will support the outside walls of the house. They also serve as connection points for floor **joists**. Joists are wooden or metal support beams that go from wall to wall. But most joists do not go across the widest parts of a basement. They may reach only to a wall or steel girder between basement walls. Joists are placed about 16 inches (41 cm) apart. They provide a base for the first floor of the house.

Carpenters hammer floorboards or plywood sheets onto the joists, giving the house a first floor. The floor and foundation are now more than solid enough to hold the house's frame.

The outside wall frames are the first parts of the house to rise from the floor. They are wood "skeletons" with openings left in them for windows and doors. The main parts of the wall frames are upright "two-by-fours," 2-by-4-inch (5-by-10-cm) wood planks called studs. In some cases, the studs are 2-by-6 inch (5-by-15-cm) planks. Carpenters put wall frames together one at a time before raising them onto the floor. Once the outside walls are in place, carpenters nail the wall frames together.

The plywood sheathing of this new house has been wrapped with a wind and rain-resistant plastic.

The next step is the roof frame. It, too, is constructed of wood planks. Rafters rise at an angle from wooden horizontal supports, or wall plates. They meet at a ridgeboard. The ridgeboard forms the crest, or peak, of the roof line. Some houses have several peaks, depending on the style of the house. The rafters make a triangle-shaped frame for the roof. The base of the triangle is a line of ceiling joists. They are the framework for the uppermost ceiling of the house. In houses that have attics, they are also the attic floor. A house with an open, two-story ceiling does not have attic space.

As the framework is finished, carpenters begin covering the frame with **sheathing**. Sheathing is the first layer used to cover the roof and outside walls. It can be one of several materials, including fiberboard, plasterboard, or plywood. Sheathing is nailed to the studs and rafters. It is the "skin" on the house skeleton.

With sheathing installed, workers can add a layer of tarpaper to the roof and a plastic, wind-resistant wrap to the outside walls. Flashing—pieces of sheet metal—is placed around any roof openings, such as the chimney. Flashing helps keep chimney heat away from the roof. It also provides protection against moisture entering the roof. The roof can now be covered with shingles and the walls with siding.

A carpenter stands on a ceiling joist and attaches wood brace boards to the studs that make the roof rafters.

Home siding is very different in different parts of North America. In some places brick siding is common. Frame, or wood, siding has always been popular. Aluminum siding often looks like wood siding, but it is less expensive and is easier to care for. Stone, stucco, shingles, and cement are among other products used for house siding.

Meanwhile, carpenters have built the inside wall frames. The walls separate one room from another. They are smaller versions of outside walls. Like them, they are supported by plates and joists. Doors and windows have been delivered to the home site and have been installed. If the house has a brick or stone fireplace, it has been hand-built by **masons**. The fireplace is usually constructed in a gap left in an outside wall.

With windows, doors, and fireplace in place, workers have sealed off the inside of the house from weather. Now workers can finish the inside. Some of the inside work was finished while the siding was added. Electricians ran wiring from the basement to each room in the house. Plumbers put in the copper and plastic pipes that carry water into and out of the house. The plumber also began to finish the bathroom.

Once the outside is complete, workers put in metal **ductwork**—long, boxlike tubes that weave through the walls and under the floor—for heating and air-conditioning.

Masons work from a scaffold framework to build the brick facing.

New homes have a central heater, or furnace, that blows warm air through the ductwork into each room. Most furnaces use electricity or natural gas. The air-conditioner usually shares the furnace's ductwork, but blows cold air.

Workers add insulation to the house after the basic home systems are in place. Insulation is placed in the ceiling framework and in the wall frames. It fills every space in the wall frames with fire-resistant material. Insulation can be made of many different products, and it takes many different shapes. "Blankets" of fiberglass insulation are used in the wall spaces. No matter what it's made of, insulation helps keep heat in during the winter and cold air out. In warm weather, it keeps cool air in. Good insulation saves home owners energy costs.

After insulation has been installed, ceiling and wall frames can be enclosed. Wall frames are commonly finished with gypsum board, also known as dry wall. Gypsum board is heavy, but it cuts easily with a knife and can be put on quickly and neatly. Gypsum board is applied in wide sections that are trimmed to fit the wall or ceiling space. A dry-waller nails them onto studs or joists, then covers the seams between side-by-side dry wall sections with tape. Next, the dry-waller covers the tape and nail heads with spackling paste. When the paste dries, the walls are smooth and show no seams. While the dry-waller finishes, other workers put tiles in shower stalls and on some floors. Tiles are put on a dry, solid surface with a special glue. Tilers fill the gaps between the tiles with a fine, hard-drying cement called **grout**.

The plywood floor of the house may stay that way. Carpet will be added later. Or an additional, smooth wooden floor may be added. These "hardwood" floors are made of hard, long-wearing oak or maple.

Home frames are made of softer woods, like pine and hemlock. These woods can be easily sawed, **planed**, and drilled. Hardwood floors are made of straight planks that are grooved to fit tightly together. The floor planks are joined, trimmed, sanded, stained, and covered with a glossy, protective finish.

A new home awaits an owner.

A finishing carpenter will now add wooden molding to the bottoms—and sometimes the tops—of walls. The carpenter will also add cabinets. A painter will paint the walls and stain the woodwork around doors and windows.

Some people say a house is never finished, and certainly housework is an unending job. But when the painter leaves, this new home is basically complete.

GREAT AMERICAN HOUSES

Almost every town in America has homes that are historic or show fine architecture. Here are some examples of the thousands of wonderful American houses:

California – Hearst Castle, San Simeon. Publisher William Randolph Hearst built a stunning mansion of 115 rooms in the Mediterranean Revival style. Constructed between 1919-1947, it overlooks the Pacific Ocean.

Connecticut – Mark Twain House, Hartford. Famous American writer Mark Twain lived 17 years in this 19-room, Victorian Gothic home built in 1873-74.

District of Columbia – Old Stone House. Built in 1765, this is the oldest house in the capital and a fine example of pre-Revolutionary War architecture.

Florida – Oldest House, St. Augustine. This small house dates to the early 1700s with hand-made cedar beams and coquina shell walls. Its style shows both Spanish and British architecture.

Illinois – Robie House, Chicago. Frank Lloyd Wright's Robie House was finished in 1910. Neighbors thought the house was terrible, but its new design and construction made it a gem of Prairie School architecture.

Iowa – Brucemore, Cedar Rapids. This 21-room mansion, built in the 1880s, is an excellent example of Queen Anne style.

Louisiana – Nottaway Plantation, White Castle. Built in 1859, Nottaway was the largest house in Louisiana. This 3-story, 64-room mansion is a blend of Greek Revival and Italianate architecture. It is the largest remaining plantation house in the South.

Maine – Wadsworth-Longfellow House, Portland. Built in 1785-86, this was the home of General Peleg Wadsworth and the first brick home in Portland.

Maryland – Thomas Stone National Historic Site, Port Tobacco. Thomas Stone, signer of the Declaration of Independence, built this Georgian home in 1771.

Massachusetts – House of Seven Gables Historic Site, Salem. Several historic homes are here, including the 1682 Hathaway House, 1658 Retire Beckett House, and others.

New York – Kykuit, Sleepy Hollow. The Rockefellers' summer home was completed in 1913. It's a beautiful house with beautiful gardens.

North Carolina – Biltmore Estate, Asheville. Fabulous flower gardens color the grounds of this 250-room French Renaissance-style home. It was built by George Washington Vanderbilt late in the 1800s.

Pennsylvania – Cliveden, Germantown. This classic Georgian home was completed in 1767. The house shows the cannonball scars of the Battle of Germantown.

Rhode Island – The Elms, Newport. This Neoclassical mansion copied an 18th-century French residence near Paris.

South Carolina – Drayton Hall, Charleston. This plantation mansion was begun about 1738 by John Drayton. In near-original condition, the house is an excellent example of Mediterranean Revival style.

Virginia – Monticello, Charlottesville. Thomas Jefferson's famous 43-room home was built between 1769-1784, and was of Jefferson's own design.

Wisconsin – House on the Rock, Spring Green. Built in the 1940s, this multi-level house crowns chimney-like Deer Shelter Rock. It is a unique architectural wonder.

GLOSSARY

architect (AHR keh tekt) — a person who designs structures

architecture (AHR keh tek cher) — the art or science of building

asphalt (AS fawlt) — a tar-like substance

colonist (KAHL eh nist) — one of the early European settlers of England's 13 colonies in what would become the United States

contractor (KAHN trak ter) — a person or company that is hired to construct a house or part of it

ductwork (DUKT work) — a connected series of boxlike steel tubes

footing (FOOT ing) — an underground support, usually made of concrete, on which columns or walls can be set

gable (GAY bel) — the vertical, triangular end of a building

gravity (GRAV eh tee) — the force that pulls objects to the ground

grout (GROWT) — thin mortar used to fill spaces, such as those between tiles

joist (JOYST) — any of the wooden planks or metal arms that go from wall to wall to support a floor or ceiling

load (LOHD) — weight distribution throughout a structure

mason (MAY sen) — one who works with masonry products, such as bricks

masonry (MAY sen ree) — a building material such as stone, clay, brick, or concrete

permit (PER mit) — a document granting permission

planed (PLAYND) — to be smoothed out by use of a tool called a plane

rafter (RAF ter) — any of the parallel beams that support a roof

Renaissance (ren eh SAHNS) — the period from the early 14th century into the 17th century in Europe when art, science, and exploration flowered

sheathing (SHEE thing) — the first covering, usually of waterproof material, on the outside frame walls of a house

speculation (spek yeh LAY shen) — the taking of a business risk

spindlework (SPIN del work) — woodworking of long, round rods called spindles

subcontractor (sub KAHN trak ter) — a tradesperson, such as an electrician, who often works under a general contractor

surveyor (ser VAY er) — one who measures land boundaries and forms

symmetry (SIM e tree) — balanced proportions; evenness

thatch (THACH) — bundles of straw, reeds, or rushes used as part of a shelter

INDEX

Further Reading:

Armentrout, David and Patricia. *Diggers*. Rourke, 1995

Graham, Rickard. *Building Homes*. Lerner, 1989

Websites to Visit:

www.monticello.org

www.mountvernon.org

www.cr.nps.gov

www.nthp.org